THE LITTLE BOOK OF
HOT LOVE
SPELLS

THE LITTLE BOOK OF
HOT LOVE
SPELLS

SOPHIA

Sophia (signature)

**Andrews McMeel
Publishing**

Kansas City

To Shiva A. and Shakti S.,
the two hottest people I know!

THE LITTLE BOOK OF HOT LOVE SPELLS

Copyright © 2002 by Sophia. All rights reserved.
Printed in Hong Kong. No part of this book may be used or reproduced
in any manner whatsoever without written permission except
in the case of reprints in the context of reviews. For information, write
Andrews McMeel Publishing, an Andrews McMeel Universal company,
4520 Main Street, Kansas City, Missouri 64111.

02 03 04 05 06 KWF 10 9 8 7 6 5 4 3 2 1

ISBN: 0-7407-2722-2

Library of Congress Control Number: 2002102575

Book composition by Holly Camerlinck

Contents

Contents

Hot Astrology Spells

Introduction

No matter what your guiding philosophy or belief system is, life is indeed short, and we should all live our lives to the fullest, right? To many it means having the best possible time and helping as many people as possible have a great time as well here on this wonderful planet. Lots of famous people (I forget who) say that it isn't the length of one's life that is important, but the quality of that life lived. Sounds good, but I'll take both a long *and* an excellent life, please. Are you with me here?!

Which brings me to this book you have in your hot little hands!

I've published little spell books before. I've written a little book of love spells, one on hexes, another on work called *The Little Book of Office Spells*, and a garden magic book too.

These are all great things—worthwhile and lovable! Yet, as I finished my last book *(The Little Book of Money Spells),* I mused long and sweetly on this marvelous thing called magic.

I thought about all the spells I knew and all the magical people I knew and mused on what could possibly tie all those things together. I mean, what do people *want* when they turn to magic? Deep down, what are we all after when we light that candle, draw that rune, and chant that name?

One day it came to me: A spark! We want that . . . special thing. That zap, that tingle, that rush, that—love of life! In other words, we want *excitement!* A quiet love affair is never enough for us, is it? It has to be *wildly* romantic and *intense,* right? And what do we say when something that was once wonderful and exciting becomes dull and routine?

"It's lost its magic."

And what gives us that spark? That magic? Love!

Not just any old love, romantic, exciting, sizzling-*hot* love!

So I decided to write a little book of exciting spells, zap spells, tingle spells: hot spells. Spells for the young and young at heart who simply cannot abide being bored, stuck in a rut, staid, safe as milk, or complacent about life. We are surrounded by the most fantastic reality. Our world has a million wonders and all the sorrows we encounter do not dim the infinite joy available to those who have the will to open their hearts! Just telling the universe that you are ready for some hot romance will get things jumping, believe me!

This book is for you wild folks that want to open your lives to some romantic fun flames!

If some part of your life is humdrum, ho hum, repetitive, dry, gray, or boring, well, here is what I have to say: You can do something about it tonight! Move on! Move up! Try something new! *Do it* (a spell, that is)!

Oh yes, I hear it every day. Lonely clients come to me unhappy, all convinced that the sad state of affairs surrounding them is inescapable. Balderdash! You just need to light a little fire under your . . . uh . . . foundation. Throw a spark into the dry kindling of your life, toss a candle in the barbecue of your troubles. You get the idea.

Think of these hot spells as a box of magical matches, ready to light your fire. Or maybe as a big pack of different kinds of multicolored magical fireworks! Pow! Love! Bam! Romance! Womp! Unexpected thrills! Ahhhh! Ohhhhh! Doesn't that sound like fun?

And, folks, that's what life is all about: fun. Never forget that. This spell stuff is fun! Oh sure, we have lots of serious and important things we need to accomplish in our time on this planet, but we must never forget that we are also here on earth to be happy and, at least for me, being happy means being excited, and being excited means keeping things hopping, especially with that someone special! So when you are feeling blue, or stuck in a rut and listless, reach for this book! I guarantee that just reading one of these little magical red-hots will cheer you up and add some erotic sparkle to your life. Who knows what will happen if you actually start *doing* them? Gosh, your love life could improve, your excursions could get more exciting, romance might lurk in every shadow, you might start enjoying your dreams! Take control of your

life! Unhappy? Change things. Anyone can; *you* can. Bored?
Then spice things up! No need for pepper; toss one of these
little hot spells into the mix, put on some sunglasses, and watch
that spark become a flame of love love love!

Some people are *hot*.
Some are *not*.
Be hot!
—Sophia

HOT LIPS SPELL

The old song says, "A kiss is but a kiss," but, we know that isn't true, don't we?

I mean, just think of the difference between your grandmother's kiss and the last thirty-second passionate kiss you received. Both are nice, but the latter is nicer! If you haven't been getting your full allotment of hot kisses lately, try this little spell.

By the way, this is good for both sexes.
Everyone loves hot kisses!

You Will Need
+ some almond oil
+ a little rosemary (fresh if possible)
+ a small dish

The Spell
Three days before a full moon, mix the almond oil
with the rosemary, saying:

LUST AND LOVE
LOVER AND FRIEND
BRING KISSES OF PASSION
THAT NEVER END
LUDENS OS!

Let it sit until the full moon. On that night,
dip your finger in the mixture and say:

KISSES OF LOVE
KISSES OF LUST
FLY TO ME!
COME YOU MUST!
BY LUNA'S LIGHT
SO MUST IT BE
COME HOT LIPS
SET ME FREE!

When you are ready for a hot date, gently paint your lips
with a touch of this special oil.

Save the rest for later if you like.

You are now ready to go out! Whoever gets your next
hot kiss will light up like a neon sign. But be careful—
you may soon have a tiger on your hands! Grrrrr!

Hotdog Spell

See that guy on the skateboard doing a flip in the air? How about that woman snow boarder going off the cliff? And your friend the bungee jumper? Hotdogs, all of them. If you or a loved one is bold enough to do extreme sports or is extreme about any sport, you'll need this little courage/protection charm. Tie it on and fly! By the way, this works great for granting courage for blind dates or parties if you are timid!

You Will Need
+ a red strip of fabric or ribbon (natural material, about six inches long)
+ a dried oak leaf
+ a plate
+ matches
+ a permanent blue marker

THE SPELL

On a Tuesday at sunrise (or early in the morning for you sleepyheads!) crumble the oak leaf on the plate and light it. As it smokes, pass the red band through the smoke ten times, saying:

> STRONG AS AN OAK
> TOUGH AS WOOD
> FEARLESS AND STRONG
> DO WHAT YOU SHOULD!
> FORTIS!

With the blue marker, carefully draw the following runes on the red band, saying:

FORTIS FORTIS
STRONG AND FAST
BY THIS CHARM
SPIRIT EVER LAST!

Light the leaf again, pass the band through the smoke three more times, and repeat the first verse. Scatter the rest of the ashes and leaf bits outside when it has burned out.

This charm can be worn as a bracelet or anklet, or it can be tied to a glove, hat, or bicycle handlebar, for that matter! Run faster, jump higher, and play crazier—with magic!

HOT TO TROT SPELL

Have you heard people say "it was like dancing on air!" or "she's as graceful as a ballerina?" If you like dancing but aren't the best at it or you want to go out and try some wild new salsa, swing, or even mosh pit action, and you want to have fun and look good and not kill anyone, this spell is for you! It'll get those feet a-tapping and you a-laughing.

YOU WILL NEED
+ Chinese chili oil (aka hot oil—you can find it in any supermarket)
+ a small cup
+ a small, very clean or new paintbrush

THE SPELL
On a Wednesday at sunset, put a little chili oil in the cup, dip the brush in it, and turn around three times clockwise, saying:

DANCE
TRANCE
ROMANCE!

Then paint the following symbol on the soles of both
of your favorite dance shoes, saying:

LILA FILL WITH DANCE
YAKSHI EN-TRANCE
TRIPURA BRING ROMANCE!
SVAHA!

Take a taste of the oil to spice up your mood, then hit the
floor and shake that thang!

No matter how geeky you feel, everyone will love ya!
Go for it!

Hot House Spell

There is no place like home, especially if every room is
buzzing with those hot love vibes! This little spell really helps
to get things going at home, no matter what your naughty
plans might be. Set a light under those tired routines or fire up
some new ones. With this spell, home is *definitely* where
the heart is.

You Will Need
+ a little rose oil
+ small red candles for every room (beeswax is best,
but any will do)
+ a little pure water
+ a small bowl
+ matches
+ one red rose

Make sure all the candles are placed on plates
or in good holders.

THE SPELL

First, clean your house really well. Then, on a Thursday, as close
to a full moon as possible, set out the rose oil, water, small
bowl, matches, candles, and rose. Hold up your arms and say:

ISIS BRIGHT
DESCEND FROM ABOVE
FILL MY HOUSE
WITH BOUNDLESS LOVE!
TUA AST!

Then, anoint each candle heavily with rose oil and place
four drops of the oil into the bowl. Add some water,
saying all the time:

LOVE LIGHT
JOY BRIGHT
COME TONIGHT!

Keep chanting this as you light all the candles and place them in every room. When done, continue chanting, and sprinkle every room with the water-and-oil mixture, using the red rose to do so. When done, take the stem off the rose, place the blossom in the bowl in the remaining water-oil mixture, and place it on a table in the middle of your home.

Raise your arms and say:

LOVE LADY ISIS
BLESS ALL HERE
FILL ALL WITH LOVE
BANISH ALL FEAR!
TUA AST!

Let the candles burn down (keep an eye on them!) until they go out. You house is now full of the love vibe. Make it a "home sweet home"!

Hot Sauce Spell

When you are cooking, you may often want to spice up a dish just to keep it interesting. Well, romance is a lot like cooking. There are feasts and fast food, but when you need to spice things up, grab this little bottle and add a few dashes to any dish and watch the sparks fly. Prepare it once and keep it in the cupboard. You never know when you'll need it!

You Will Need
+ a small, very clean bottle
(an old salad dressing bottle is perfect)
+ three garlic cloves (peeled)
+ a cup of red-wine vinegar
+ three teaspoons of sugar
+ one large fresh jalapeño pepper
+ seven red rose petals (from a rosebush that has not been
sprayed with any chemicals!)

THE SPELL
On a very sunny Friday, assemble all your ingredients
in a very sunny place near noon.

Wave the garlic cloves 'round your ingredients;
drop them in the bottle and say:

BEGONE ALL GLOOM
BEGONE ENNUI

Pour in the red-wine vinegar and say:

COME O FIRE
OF DESIRE
SO MAY IT BE!

Drop in the sugar, saying:

MAKE IT SWEET
MAKE IT NICE

Kiss and gently bite the jalapeño sensuously,
thinking naughty thoughts, drop it in and say:

GIVE IT SPARKS
GIVE IT SPICE!

Add the rose petals. Then put the top on
and shake it up, saying:

VENUS BONUM
FILL WITH ZEST
SPICE IT UP!
AMORE EST!

This makes a great salad dressing, addition to any meat dish,
or . . . well, use your imagination! A lovely gift as well! Keeps
forever, and remember, a little romantic sauce perks up any
savory "dish," no matter who it is!

HOT LOVE TIP SPELL

Where is your intuition when you need it? You have, shall we
say, strong feelings for someone, but how does he feel about
you? What can you do to get him interested in you? You need
that intuition to kick in and help out! Unfortunately, your
crystal ball is out of commission, but this spell will help.
Here is how to get a psychic hot tip on how to hook
this potential lover.

YOU WILL NEED
+ flowing water (a creek is best)
+ an item that relates to the person you are seeking a tip
about (a letter? snip of hair? picture?)
+ a steel needle
+ matches

The Spell

On a Monday morning, when the moon is waxing, go to the flowing water. Hold the significant item in your left hand and the needle in your right hand, pointing away from you. Then, turn about while holding the needle pointing out, saying:

> Out about
> Compass spin
> Point me now
> To look within

Light a match and heat the tip of the needle just until the part of the needle you are holding gets warm—very little! Say:

> Flame and point
> Water and sight
> Give me inspiration
> By this night
> Make my love
> Hot and bright
> Ignis spiritus!

Then, clear your mind, drop the needle into the water,
and let go.

Stare with unfocused eyes into the water, thinking about the
one you are hot for, and set your mind free. You will receive
many new insights about your potential lover—things he likes,
favorite colors, and so on. A number of real intuitive flashes
will come to you. Now go and act on those flashes! Did you
"see" that person with yellow roses? Buy some and give them
to that person. Act on your intuition and sparks will fly!

HOT OFFICE ROMANCE SPELL

Yes, we know it is clichéd, but it is still as true today as it was
a decade ago: Office romances are hot! Maybe it's all that hard
work you are putting in together, or those feverish
presentations and projects. Anyway, if you are looking for a
little hot romance in the office, try this spell. You can visualize
one person you have your eye on, or cast your net wide and
see who comes to your call!

YOU WILL NEED
+ an old dry maple leaf
+ a bowl or plate
+ a small piece of lapis lazuli (it can be in a ring,
earring, bracelet, etc.)
+ a little writing (a simple job ad for your dream
office date in a few short lines—hard copy)
+ matches

THE SPELL

On a Tuesday at dawn (or close to it), face east and, closing
your eyes, see the red and yellow sun shining into your body,
filling you with the will to move on or up at work.

Place the leaf in the bowl, the stone or jewelry in the leaf,
then take the "ad" you've written, read it aloud, and light it on
fire. Let the burning paper fall on the stone/leaf. The dry leaf
should also burn, at least in part.

As it smolders, say:

My will is a flame
My will is a sun
Bring love to work
I am the one
I will to find love
To move forward
Exceed
In whatever I will

I SOON WILL SUCCEED!
THELEMA!

Pick up the stone and hold it up to the rising sun. Feel it fill
with the power of your will to find that office romance (if the
sun is not visible, do so in your mind's eye). Then say:

THELEMA FIAT
SO MAY IT BE
LOVE COME TO ME
AND SO I AM FREE!

Place the stone in a pocket or put on the jewelry and go out
and find that hot office romance!

Hottie Spell

It's not that you're picky, it just comes down to a simple fact. You just want to find someone of your own species. Is that too much to ask for? This is a fun spell to do with friends, too. The more who participate, the greater the chances that your "hottie hunting" will be a success!

You Will Need
+ a red pen
+ a little cayenne pepper
+ a piece of red paper (about five inches long)
+ a ceramic or glass dish
+ matches

THE SPELL
Do this before hottie hunting, whenever that is, in a place
where you won't be bothered (especially if you are going to do
this with a bunch of giggly friends!).

With the red pen, draw this figure on the paper, saying:

HEAT TO HEAT
EMBER TO EMBER
BRING US LOVE
WE'LL ALWAYS REMEMBER
KLIM LILA !

Sprinkle the cayenne pepper over the symbol and then
roll or twist the paper into a tube. Place the tube
of paper in the dish.

Light one end on fire and let it burn down and smolder. With your hands, push the smoke over your head, heart, and lower body. Feel that love vibe clear away everything standing between you and a hottie! Say:

> LOVE AND MIRTH
> PASSION BE MINE
> OPEN RED DOORS
> LET LOVE SHINE!

Put just a grain of cayenne pepper on your tongue. Whoooo! Shiver and shake and go out hottie hunting. The gods of love will mysteriously guide you to places of hottie abundance as you go out to play. Have fun and always play safe!

HOT HUNT SPELL

This is it. You are going in for the kill, and you are going to be
successful—well, with my help! You want that special person.
Meow! You must have him or her. You are burning with desire
for him or her, but he or she is hard to romantically reach.
What can you do? Go on the prowl, you tiger, you.
Do this spell and pounce.

YOU WILL NEED
+ some cat fur (just a little—don't hurt the cat!)
+ some of your hair
+ a little catnip (dried)
+ a small matchbox or other container
+ matches
+ a small plate

THE SPELL

Place all the ingredients except a little of the catnip into the container or matchbox on a Thursday at midnight near a full moon. Mix them together, thinking about the one you desire, and say:

> FELINE FURY
> FEED THE FIRE
> A PREDATOR AM I
> I GAIN MY DESIRE
> SA-SEKHEM!

Breathe into it three times, whisper the name of the one you desire, and close it.

Burn a little of the catnip in the plate and wave the charm through it three times, saying:

> AH SA-SEKHEM!

Now, leap from your position!

Run out and keep the charm on you and roar as you do it! Go find that object of desire and turn on all the charm. Don't give up. Woo him or her. You know what to do.

Go get 'em, tiger!

Hotcake Spell

Good morning! This is a spell for all you early birds. As the old folk rhyme goes, "The early bird gets the . . ." Hmmm. Well, you know what I mean. Do you desire a special romantic wake-up call from your late riser? Want to hook someone into being a late-riser with you? This old family recipe will help you both start out the day just right. Breakfast never tasted so good.

You Will Need
+ simple complete pancake mix (make it a nice mix!)
+ a half-teaspoon of fresh ginger
+ a half-teaspoon of fresh cinnamon
+ a half-teaspoon of fresh nutmeg

The Spell
Follow the directions on the box, then add the spices to the batter, one at a time, saying the following:

Add the ginger and say:

SHAKTI SPICE
BLESS THE CAKE

Add the cinnamon and say:

SHAKTA SPICE
GREAT POWER MAKE

Add the nutmeg and say:

SVAHA SPICE
SERPENT FIRE
SHAKE!

Stir the batter as fast and furiously as you can with lots of really smutty thoughts and images dancing through your head.

Cook and serve. Then look out!

Hot Looks Spell

It is the age-old question: why do some of us always look great and others look like something the cat dragged in? You are unable to hide what you need to conceal, and accent what makes you look good. It's just not fair that others can show up in anything and look drop-dead gorgeous. This ancient spell for beauty will make you glow inside and out. Just snap your little fingers if you want to look and feel hot, hot, hot.

You Will Need
+ a real silver or silver-plated bowl or plate (it must be cleaned well and very shiny)
+ a bottle of very pure mineral water from a snowy or glacier area

+ a lime
+ a small knife (silver if possible, but not steel or iron)
+ a sprig of fresh rosemary
+ a small clean bottle with a top

The Spell

On the night of a full moon, wearing as many white clothes as
you can, go to a quiet, natural outdoors place (if possible)
where you can see the moon. Place the silver bowl in the
moonlight and then pour the water into it. Stare at the
reflection of the moon in the plate until it is perfectly still,
then say:

Aradia luna
I draw thee down
Into the well
Of beauty and light
Bless me with beauty
O queen of the night!

Cut the lime in half with the silver knife and place the two
halves face down in the water, side by side. Place the sprig
of rosemary between them. Say:

BEAUTY OF LIGHT
CLING TO ME
BEAUTY OF NIGHT
LET ALL BEAUTY SEE!
ARARITA!

Leave the plate in the moonlight for at least one hour.

Then, throw away the lime and sprig and put the moon-water
in the bottle. Wash your face with a handful of it and the
moon-glamor will cling to you. You will be the glamorous
creature all know you to be, like a rose in moonlight!

Keep this water in the dark always and pat on a bit
when you want to really cast that spell!

Hot Damn Spell

Unforgettable, that's what you are . . . hotter than blue blazes and steam heat. Slowly you enter the party and everyone's mouths drop open. The guests whisper to each other, "Who is this divine creature?" Now is the time to really shake everyone up. Tonight is the night when you can make sure that nobody will ever forget you—if you use this.

You Will Need
+ a small vial of jasmine oil (as pure as you can find)
+ a garnet (or a ruby if you can afford it!)

The Spell
On a Friday at sunset, take out the oil and drop three drops onto the ground.

Then massage some oil into your forehead, throat,
and heart, saying:

HRIM AND SHRIM AND KRIM TO THEE
LET ALL EYES TURN NOW TO ME!

Rub some on the garnet, saying:

SPARK IS LIT
SPIRIT BURN
MAKE IT BRIGHT
ALL EYES TURN!

Clap your hands three times and keep the garnet (or ruby)
close to your flesh.

Keep this stone with you whenever you want to be really
noticed—and wear the perfume oil as well. If you get too
much attention, toss the garnet in moving water
to break the spell.

HOT ART-OF-LOVE SPELL

What is sexier that making art with or for your sweetheart?
Poems in the moonlight! Gentle watercolor paintings in the
bedroom! Handmade charms, toys, clothes! Nothing says
"I love you" better than romantic art. Everyone is creative
when they are filled with love; you don't have to be Picasso to
create something that casts an artistic spell on someone.
Try this spell to inspire you and to help you create
something to delight your honey!

You Will Need
+ a die (one of a pair of dice)
+ some correction fluid
+ a black marker pen
+ a bottle of plum wine
+ a glass

THE SPELL

On a new moon, mark out the dots on the die with correction fluid and let it dry, then write the following symbols on the six sides of the die:

Pour a small glass of the plum wine, take a big sip, and sprinkle some on the die, saying:

> TENJIN-SAMA
> HEAR MY PLEA
> OPEN THE GATE
> OF CREATIVITY
> LOVE THROUGH ART
> SO MAY IT BE!
> HU!

Shake the die in your cupped hands and then toss it.

Depending on what symbol appears, do the following,
always thinking about your sweetheart!:

Go out and dance or do strenuous exercise. ╋

Sit and meditate in complete silence. ○

Make or listen to music for one hour. ⊚

Go and do something erotic. △

Go and eat and drink something wonderful, paying complete
attention to your feast. ☐

Go play and laugh outrageously about something. ✳

After doing this spell, still thinking of your sweetheart, now
full of creativity, make something beautiful to give him
or her, or do something artistic with him or her!
The art will be full of love!

HOT WATER SPELL

Sometimes getting into hot water is bad, but sometimes getting into hot water is very, very good. Here is a little romance spell to induce hot sweats and steam even before the bathtub is filled! For use alone or with that very special partner . . . Try this one and enjoy making a mess out of the bathroom.

You Will Need
+ dried lavender
+ dried basil
+ dried rose petals
+ a small muslin (cloth) bag
+ a piece of string to tie it closed
(if it doesn't have a drawstring)
+ a nice red candle
+ matches

The Spell
Put the dried herbs in the muslin bag and place it in the tub.
Run very hot water over it, saying:

> Like and love and lust
> I call thee to me
> Flesh, heat, and steam
> I bind these three!
> Cauldron of desire
> Flow and set me free!
> Amat est!

Light the candle and turn off the lights. Let the steam envelop
you as the herbs steep in the bath. When you are ready, get in
and (if this is a joint operation) pull your friend in with you.
Whisper erotically:

> Flesh, heat, and steam
> Let this be a dream
> Here a love supreme

Have a lot of fun . . . don't worry about getting clean!

And you will smell so nice afterward you will attract
all sorts of attention!

HOT BED SPELL

One can always catch up on their forty winks—besides, why go
to sleep when you have someone fantastic lying beside you? If
you don't, then you need to get someone in there pronto!
Tantalizing, enticing, love can be brought to a new climatic
high with a little bit of bed magic. To spice up any love life try
this old gypsy secret.

YOU WILL NEED
✦ a real wishbone from a chicken or turkey
that has been eaten in a loving atmosphere
(boil the wishbone very well then clean and dry it completely
before doing this spell!)
✦ red thread

THE SPELL

On a full moon at midnight, sit on the bed you wish to charge
up and hold the wishbone, one "branch" in each hand, so it is
pointing up. Holding it like this, point it to each direction
and say the following:

West:
KISSES SWEET
WHEN WE MEET
ADA ME KAMAV!

North:
EMBRACES STRONG
LASTING LONG
ADA ME KAMAV!

East:
WORDS SO FINE
CARESSES LIKE WINE
ADA ME KAMAV!

South:
HEAT AND FIRE
ALL I DESIRE!
ADA ME KAMAV!

Then bind the red thread 'round the top of the wishbone,
clockwise, eleven times, saying each time:

ADA ME KAMAV!

Place the charm under the mattress and let it do its work.
Ooh la la!

Hot Potato Spell

Liven up your inner spud and stop being such a couch potato! This is for both of you! It's to exercise romance and beef up that libido. Help heat your lovable spud into a steaming hot potato with all the trimmings!

You Will Need
+ a few fresh oak leaves
+ five acorns
+ a ceramic plate
+ matches

The Spell
First, place the oak leaves about the house, in all the places where you spud-out (under sofa cushions is a must), and let them dry for a few days. Then, on a Thursday when the home is empty, take all the leaves and lightly crumble

them on the plate. Place the acorns on top and then light
the leaves on fire, saying:

LIGHTNING THUNDER
OAK OF EARTH
OVER AND UNDER
BRING NEW BIRTH
TYR TOR TYR!

Carry the plate with smoldering leaves into every room and
then back to the center of the home. When the embers burn
out, take the acorns out and dust them off, then hide them in
places about the house where you want to be more "active"
with your partner (there is that sofa again) . . .

Finally, take the ashes outside and dump them on your
doorstep or around your house. Using the ashes
make this figure:

You will have a lovely lively time in the near future!

Your house is now a very, very, very nice house.

RED HOTS SPELL

Projecting that old "red hots" vibe and "that old black magic" will have your intended victim under your spell, no matter if you are Spiderwoman or Spiderman. The web you weave with this hot spell will catch any fly. Once you've got your lover in your clutches, he or she will surrender to your sweet venom.

You Will Need
+ a jar of pure honey
+ large, whole, dried red hot peppers
(found in any grocery store)
+ a picture or something touched by your "intended"

The Spell
On a Sunday at midday, take the items to a sunny spot
outside near a tree.

Dig a small hole near the tree and pour in a small amount
of honey. Cover it with dirt, saying:

> MAGNA GAIA
> HEAR MY PLEA
> SWEETEN THE LOVE
> OF THE ONE I SEE.
> (Visualize your "intended.")

Push six of the dried peppers into the rest of the honey
in the jar, and say:

> SUN AND MOON
> GOLD AND RED
> BEAR TO HONEY
> LOVER IN MY BED
> LASHTAL!

Then leave the jar of honey outside for the rest of the day, in
the sunlight if possible.

Then, at sunset, tape the picture of the intended or the item the intended has touched to the jar facing the jar. Then hold it tight and eat some of the hot honey with a spoon, silently repeating the last verse to yourself, visualizing your intended.

Do this each night at sunset for as long as it takes, until that one is *yours!*

If he or she doesn't come and the honey is gone, it is not meant to be. Move on.

If your intended does fall into your arms, feed him or her the rest of the honey in a special dessert! Bzzzzzzz!

HOT SHOT O' LOVE SPELL

Love Potion Number . . . Nine. We all know the song, but does it really exist? I don't have the recipe for Love Potion Number Nine, but I do have the secret recipe for Love Potion Number Ten, which is the new and improved, slightly updated version of number nine. And it gets you tipsy! Be careful, a little bit goes a long way. One shot glass full may be all you need to set the night afire!

YOU WILL NEED
+ a bottle of very good vodka or rum
+ a small raw jalapeño pepper
+ a stalk of fresh basil
+ a vanilla bean
+ a straight pin

The Spell
Under a full moon, open the bottle of liquor
and take a small mouthful.

Spray-spit a little to the ground to the four directions and say:

Honor to the spirits
Honor to love
Bring out the powers
From below and above!
Ashe!

Take the pin and stick it through the pepper and the vanilla
bean so they are joined together, saying:

Grand erzulie
Lady of love
Bring romance to me
From below and above!
Ashe!

Put them into the liquor bottle along with the basil. Put the top on and dance wildly in a clockwise circle, all the while shaking the bottle like mad!

When exhausted, beam all that lusty energy into it and say:

> THE SPELL
> IS DONE
> LOVE IS MINE
> PRAISE TO THE LADY
> AND SPIRITS DIVINE!
> ASHE!

Take a swig, offer a few drops on the ground to Erzulie, Goddess of Love, then go home and put that potion away until you have a chance to use it on some unsuspecting object of desire! A couple of shots will do it! Put it in a mixed drink or serve it straight up. It will be a memorable love buzz!

Hot Tamale Spell

Sizzle and pop! Want to turn a simple dinner or party into a love feast hotter than the center of the earth? Try this favorite Brujo spell from south of the border.

You Will Need

+ all the fixings for tamales or burritos (Make sure there is plenty of fresh garlic and fresh tomatoes. Set the corn tortillas aside; they are the key to the spell.)
+ a block of sweet baking chocolate
+ toothpicks

The Spell

At midnight on a Friday, before you are going to serve the charged food items, lay out as many of the soft corn tortillas as you will need for your victim(s). Heat as much of the

chocolate as you like on a small plate. Heat it just a little so it
is still solid but a bit soft.

When ready, use a toothpick to draw a heart on each tortilla
with the chocolate. When you are done, say:

HACER FELIZ
LA SEÑORA DE LA LUNA
HACER LA CORAZÓN
DIOSA! MAGNIFICA
ADELANTE!

Now, cover your lips with the slightly softened chocolate and
put a big kiss-mark in the middle of each tortilla! Put all your
love into those sweet kisses and think steamy thoughts! When
done, eat the rest of the chocolate and make those tamales or
burritos. Make sure the chocolate side is facing inward when
you roll them; none of the chocolate must show.

Serve hot and when done, get hotter still. Whoa!
Like fire for chocolate!

Hot Rub Spell

There's nothing like a little sensual massage to create some hot friction. It doesn't matter whether your preferred massage style is Swedish, Thai, or Hawaiian. This fun little spell will make it much more enjoyable, and I bet you didn't think that was possible.

You Will Need
+ a bottle of very basic massage oil (jojoba is excellent)
+ small amounts of pure rose oil, sandalwood oil, and musk oil (available anyplace that sells scented oils)
+ a small piece of rose quartz

The Spell
On a full moon or at least a waxing moon, at sunset, add the three scented oils to the bottle of massage oil. Don't add more than a half ounce of each. Take your time and combine the

scents the way you prefer. You may have more of one oil than another—it is up to you.

When done, hold up the bottle and say:

LOVE OF BODY
LOVE OF MIND
LOVE OF SPIRIT
LOVE DIVINE!
AMPLEXOR!!!

Drop the rose quartz into the bottle and breathe all your love into the potion. Then cap it and shake it while saying three times:

AMPLEXOR
CONTINGERE AMOR!

Leave the oil in the sun for a few hours to heat gently. Shake again, then store it.

Later, when you offer a massage to someone special, light a few candles, open the bottle and let that person take a deep sniff before you begin. Ah! Isn't it enchanting? They will be putty in your hands!

Hot Spot Spell

So, you're all dressed up and ready to paint the town red! But where to go? Ah! The eternal dilemma. You get out the local entertainment mag and see several possibilities. But which one will be hot? Where will the action be best? Well, ask the cosmos! This little spell will help you find your hot spot for the night!

You Will Need
+ three coins that have been thrown in a fire or cooked on a stove until black
+ a local entertainment newspaper or magazine with your three or so possible hot spots circled in red
+ a glass of red wine

The Spell
Dip the three coins in the red wine, saying:

HEAT OF FIRE
HEAT OF LUST
GRANT OUR DESIRE
GUIDE US YOU MUST!
PATERE EST!

Drink some of the wine.

Shake the three coins in your right hand and point to one of your circled choices in the magazine with your left, then drop the coins on the magazine.

Heads = Hot, Tails = Not

The more heads that are up, the hotter the place!

Do the same for each of your possible places to party and see which one produces three "heads up." This is the hottest spot for the night—go and have a blast! And keep those coins safe for next weekend!

Hot Springs Spell

Hot springs conjure up images of quiet mountain retreats and hidden romantic spas. A secret love shack is sometimes too far away when the mood strikes you. You can recapture the magic moment with a little bathroom sorcery and this spell. Sit back, relax, and soak yourself in your own private spa. Hot water takes on a whole different meaning when you blow out the candles. This can be used for romantic, erotic footbaths or baths in general.

You Will Need
+ fresh pine or fir needles from seven different trees, gathered at midnight on a Monday
+ a glass jar with lid
+ a box of sea salt

THE SPELL
Gently gather the pine needles, one handful from each tree,
then hug the tree and say:

FILL WITH LIFE
EVERGREEN MAN
FILL WITH LUST
IO PAN!

Take the needles home and fill the jar with alternating layers
of needles and salt until it is full, then breathe into it
seven times, saying:

BREATH OF LIFE
DO WHAT YOU CAN
SPRING OF LOVE
IO PAN!

Let the salts sit for one week. On the next Monday at
midnight, open the jar and sprinkle the contents onto a sheet

of paper. Then take out all the dried needles and bury them at the foot of a pine or fir tree. Put all the now sweet-smelling salts back into the jar and keep the top on tight. Use whenever you want to incite a little lust or turn a footbath into oh so much more. When you add it to bath water, whisper seven times:

İ☉ ΡΑΠ!

Ah! Hot springs eternal!

HOT MEAL SPELL

Boil and bubble, toil and trouble, cauldron brew seductive desires! With just a wave of your hands and the right ingredients you can create an aphrodisiac-meal that can send you both into orbit. So shake and bake, and fry up a lot of lovin' in the oven with this sinfully tasteful spell.

This works best with a meat, seafood, or poultry dish, though tofu can be used.

YOU WILL NEED
+ a yellow candle
+ matches
+ a fresh small yellow hot pepper
+ a fresh basil plant

THE SPELL

On a full moon, take a shower and get very clean, then go out
and do some brisk exercise, anything is fine. While doing this
you must think very romantic thoughts about your intended or
whoever is going to eat this highly charged meal.

When you finish this exercise, come back, strip off your
clothes, light the candle, put the pepper gently in your mouth
(don't bite!), and whisper:

> TRE BACT CAV
> TRE BACT ME PİYAV
> KAΠA TU MAΠGE SAL!

Then take the basil branch and gently rub it all over your
body, thinking (as the spell says) that you will both eat and
drink your luck and, with it, find love!

Take the pepper out of your mouth and then wrap it with the
basil branch and put it in the fridge (you will need to use it

within a few days). When ready, bake or fry the hot meal and
season it with the basil and hot pepper, finely chopped.
Serves: a hot time!

Once a person has had a taste of you, they will be
wanting more . . . yum!

I'm Hot Spell

Striking out lately? Something missing? Could it be . . . burning love? If you have drifted into the gray zone, never fear, this spell will light a fire under you and get you revved up! The trick is to use your heat wisely and not get scorched by some unfortunate romantic accident. This is a spell to make you an all-consuming desirable, fiery, scarlet women. Get out of that rut and blast off! Get hot!

You Will Need
+ a nice spicy-scented red candle in a holder
+ an iron or steel nail

The Spell
On a Tuesday at midnight, when the moon is waxing, find a quiet place and put the candle on the floor. Walk clockwise around the candle, holding the nail pointing out, saying:

OUT GOES WATER, EARTH, AND AIR
HERE I CALL THE FIRE FAIR!

Light the candle, saying:

FIRE MY BODY
FIRE MY HAIR
FIRE MY HEART
FIRE I SHARE
IGNIS FIAT!

Scratch this rune on the candle with the nail and say:

BABALON FIAT
NEED-FIRE BE
A FLAMING STAR
SET ME FREE!
SHINE FOREVER
A PART OF ME!

Snuff the flame with your fingers and inhale. "See" the fire
enter you and burn in your heart. Keep the nail with you
when you go out, and light this candle every time you are
feeling low and need a "power boost"! This spell will light up
your life and give you more personal power to do your will!

Hot Dreams Spell

This hot spell is to inspire exotic night fancies: Arabian nights, a full moon, and the air perfumed with roses! This secret Egyptian spell will cast you into the sky of smoldering dreams, bathing you in a new light, and help you find your love in dreamland. Don't dream it, be it.

You Will Need
+ rosewater
+ nine marigold flowers
+ a small red glass or ceramic bowl or cup

You may also bring a token of a special love to bed with you, if that is what (or whom) you wish to dream about.

The Spell
Before you go to bed, place the "love token" (if you wish to focus on a particular person or relationship) under your

pillow. Then, pour rosewater into the bowl. Take the nine marigold flowers and dip them into the water. Lightly sprinkle the rosewater around your bed in a clockwise direction using a flower, saying:

AAU NU T PET
AAU NU T PET
AAU NU T PET
NUIT, GODDESS OF STARS
OPEN THE SKY OF DREAMS!

Drop the flowers into the bowl with the rosewater and place it under the bed (or next to it if that isn't possible), saying:

A KA DUA NUIT!

Fall asleep breathing deeply and focusing on your desire. Visualize the romance you want to know about clearly and prepare for a tunnel of love dream! Buckle your dream seatbelt! Dream on!

HOT COFFEE SPELL

Nothing wakes us up like that first shot of caffeine—well, maybe one other thing is as effective . . . However, some people need caffeine in the A.M., even before any loving thoughts and this little spell combines them both, yum! All you need is a love interest to experiment with! Coffee, tea, *and* me!

YOU WILL NEED
+ three shelled almonds (plain)
+ a knife
+ coffee (you can use strong black tea or chai if you like)
+ a cinnamon stick

THE SPELL
At dawn, before you make the coffee, take the almond and scratch your initials on them with the knife, one letter for each almond, saying:

THREE NAMES I HAVE
THREE SEEDS OF PASSION
THREE HEARTS I OFFER
ONE CHARM I FASHION!
TRISHUL!

If you grind your own beans, and you should, then grind the
nuts with them and brew the coffee as you normally would. If
you don't grind your beans, then crush the almonds with a
spoon as you can and add them to the grounds. As the coffee
is brewing, scratch the initials of your intended on the
cinnamon stick, saying:

THREE NAMES YOU HAVE
THREE SEEDS OF PASSION
THREE HEARTS I CALL
ONE CHARM I FASHION!
TRISHUL!

Pour the coffee into the cup, add what your sweetheart likes,
and then stir it three times with the cinnamon stick and serve
it with the cinnamon stick in it. Soon the right sort of trouble
should be brewing and your sweetie will be
espresso-ing love for you!

HOT ROCKS SPELL

Want to get your rocks off? Well, first you have to put them on, right? Not only is this a really exotic spell but it is a fantastic massage technique that will turn even the coldest lover with a heart of stone into warm flesh in your fingers. Rock and roll!

YOU WILL NEED
+ three fist-size, very smooth, dry stones found by you. They should be fairly flat so they can comfortably be placed on a person's back.
+ three pennies
+ some sandalwood oil
+ some massage oil

The Spell

As you find the stones, leave a penny in the dirt or sand
where you find them.

Clean the stones thoroughly with a damp cloth and let them
dry for a few days in a warm spot.

Charge up and use the stones when the moon is close to full.
Any day is fine.

Massage sandalwood oil into each rock, saying one of the
following verses for each of the three:

Tamas
Moon power
Love thought
Flower

sattvas
Sun power
Love feeling
Flower

Rajas
FIRE POWER
LOVE SPARK
FLOWER

Then, very slowly heat the stones in an oven until they are hot, but not unpleasantly so.

Give your friend a lovely massage with your sandalwood-scented hands and some of the massage oil. At the end, carefully place the first stone on the back of their neck, place the second a little below the shoulder blades and the third stone at the base of the spine. Ahhhhhh! After a bit, feel free to move the stones around to sore spots that may need a little TLC. Heat and repeat until your friend drips off the table. Remember, extreme gratitude is a good thing!

Hot Momma Spell

We all get older and (shudder!) mature. Okay, not all of us mature, but we all do age and it generally sucks, right? Once simple things would have driven us wild and feeling *hot hot hot,* but sometimes, as you get along, it takes a little more juice to get the motor revved up. Well, since most perfumes come in men's and women's scents now, I'm offering his and hers jump-start kits. And remember, age is a state of mind. Old farts come in any age and all can benefit from a jolt or two.

You Will Need
+ a red candle
+ matches
+ a pair of very sexy underwear that the hot momma
will actually wear
+ a small bottle of gardenia oil

THE SPELL
On Tuesday night at midnight, near a full moon,
light the candle and say:

> MATER IGNIS
> LADY OF FIRE
> OPEN YOUR HEART
> TO LUST AND DESIRE!
> AMAT

Then pass the underwear quickly through the flame of the
candle five times. Then loosen the cap of the oil vial and heat
the vial over the flame carefully. When you can feel it
is warm, say:

> MATER IGNIS
> five times:

And then put some of the oil on the underwear in five places.
Give these as a gift or wear them yourself. Stand back and be
ready to fan the flames of passion!

Hot Daddy Spell

You Will Need
+ a red candle
+ matches
+ a pair of very sexy underwear that this hot daddy
  will actually wear!
+ a small bottle of clove oil

The Spell
On Tuesday night at midnight, near a full moon, light the
candle and say:

Pater ignis
Lord of fire
Open your heart
To lust and desire!
Amo!

Then pass the underwear quickly through the flame of the candle five times. Then loosen the cap of the oil vial and heat the vial over the flame carefully. When you can feel it is warm, say:

PATER IGNIS
five times:

And then put some of the oil on the underwear in five places. Give these later as a gift or wear them yourself. Stand back and be ready to feed the fires of desire!

Hot Rod Spell

A home may be a person's castle, but a car is a person's chariot! Hi Ho, Silver, away! If you don't have a naturally hot car, this little spell will do the trick. It will turn a lemon into a love machine. Be careful and watch those hills and curves . . .

You Will Need
+ some fresh mint
+ a small pine cone
+ a small covered basket or sachet that can be hung
from the rearview mirror

The Spell
On a hot full moon, sleep with the mint one night
and think hot rod thoughts . . .

Early the next morning, wrap the mint around the pine cone and stick it in the basket or satchel. Close it, whirl it around your head, and say:

> Winds of zain
> Chariot of cheth
> Hot love in motion
> Enjoyment: teth!

Hang it from the mirror and drive off somewhere exotic right away! Blast the right music and for goodness' sake, when it begins to really work, pull off the road before smooching!

Hot Marriage Spell

Hey, let me tell you, and my husband agrees, you don't have to be single to be *hot!* In fact, bigger bonfires take longer to burn out, baby! If you are about to enter into a hot marriage or want to heat yours up, try this little number.

You Will Need
+ two rings (gold is traditional) that the couple will wear
+ a very long piece of strong grass you pick together
+ a nice white candle
+ matches

The Spell
Go somewhere special and tie the rings together with the grass—be careful and don't rip the grass! Light the candle and, with both of you holding the grass, dangle the rings over the fire so that the flame licks them both, then say:

Not two but one
Till life is gone
We are one flame
We are one song

Take the rings out of the flame, let them cool, then separate them. Each person should put a ring on his or her partner, while both say:

For he is ever a sun and she a moon
But to him is the winged secret flame
And to her the stooping starlight

Kiss. You know, really really *kiss.* Now, go spend the rest of your lives loving and pleasing each other!

HOT DAY SPELL

A delightful day with sunny romance, beautiful places to go, exciting joys, and everything effortlessly falling into place like a long slow, sunny sail. Ah! We all know that the difference between a "perfect day" and an utter mess can be something as simple as a poorly timed hug, a dirty picnic area, or a hundred other bothersome things! This spell will not only make the day go great but will add an extra zing to make it memorable.

YOU WILL NEED
+ a small vial of lemon or lemon flower perfume or oil
+ something gold you wear
+ an orange or other light fruit with seeds

THE SPELL

Find a windowsill facing south, and place the three items on it as the sun is rising. Before you get dressed to go out, open the window, daub some of the perfume all over and say:

> SPIRIT OF THE DAYLIGHT
> SPIRIT OF ROMANCE AND LOVE
> OF THE BRILLIANT AND BRIGHT
> AND DELIGHT
> SUNLIGHT
> RAIN FROM ABOVE!
> LUX DEUS!

Rub some of the oil on the gold item and put it on. Slowly and sensuously eat the orange and carefully toss three of the seeds out the window saying:

> LUX DEUS, LICENTIA EST!

Go wash up, get dressed, and have the hot day of your life. Sizzle!

Hot Night Spell

A sultry evening with glittering chandeliers, perfect clothes, romantic sparkle, and everything effortlessly falling into place like a long slow waltz. Ah! We all know that the difference between a "perfect evening" and an utter mess can be something as simple as a poorly timed kiss, a smoky restaurant, or a hundred other bothersome things! This spell will not only make the evening go smoothly but will add an extra "oomph" to it to make it memorable.

You Will Need
+ a small vial of gardenia perfume or oil
+ something silver you wear
+ a plum or dark grape with a pit

THE SPELL

Find a windowsill facing north and place the three items on it
as the sun is setting. Before you get dressed to go out, open
the window, daub some of the perfume on, and say:

SPIRIT OF THE NIGHT
SPIRIT OF ROMANCE AND LOVE
OF SHADOWS AND DELIGHT
STARLIGHT
RAIN FROM ABOVE!
NOX DEA!

Rub some of the oil on the silver item and put it on.
Slowly and sensuously eat the plum or grape and carefully
toss the pit out the window saying:

NOX DEA, LICENTIA EST!

Go wash up, get dressed, and have the hot night of your life.
Shazam!

Hot Time Out Spell

Going out on the town for a show or event can be very erotic, if you do it right. This little spell is to inspire you, to open you and to set you on creative fire so you can mingle with the artists and literati and so you can get hot on the art of it all! A creative person is a deep and sexy person. Go forth and be art!

You Will Need
+ a few pieces of dried lavender
+ a small plate
+ matches
+ a small piece of clean amber

THE SPELL

You can do this spell anytime, but it works best when the
moon is waxing and at twilight, when artistic visions
and feelings creep out.

Sit quietly and gaze out at the twilight. Open your mind
to the romantic art vibe.

Crush the lavender and take a deep sniff. Let it fill you with
delight and inspire you! Now, toss nine small bits of lavender
aroiund you, going clockwise, saying:

CLIO! EUTERPE! MELPOMENE! TERPSICHORE!
ERATO! POLYHYMNIA! THALIA! URANIA! CALLIOPE!
DAUGHTERS OF ZEUS, MUSES OF CULTURE, INSPIRE ME!
FIRE ME! DESIRE ME!
IO MOUSAI! IO EVOEE!

Then burn some of the lavender on the plate while waving the
amber through the smoke nine times. Place it under your

tongue. Sit quietly for a minute in silence and let your imagination drift with artistic erotic fancies. When the lavender has stopped smoldering, toss the ashes into the air outside and clean off the amber.

That amber is now a special gem of inspiration that will make you artsy, sexy, and eloquent! Van Gogh forth and use your new burst of exotic erotic artistry!

Hot Music Spell

Music has made us wild and hot since the earliest worshippers of Dionysus, the Greek god of wine and pleasure, sent roving bands of crazies over the hills of Greece with buckets of vino and drums and pipes! This little spell is to add a little bass to the woofer of your love! You can use it to eroticize a CD, tape, or musical instrument.

You Will Need
+ a small red votive candle on a small saucer
+ a musical object (tape, CD, etc.)
+ matches
+ a knife
+ a piece of ginger

The Spell

On a Thursday, place the candle and saucer on the musical item to be blessed. Light the candle. Cut the ginger in half and place the pieces on either side. Say:

Ashe ashe!
Shango fill
This musical tool
With love and will
Ashe ashe!

Now, dance around the item, candle, and ginger. Dance clockwise and dance as wildly as you can. See your lover dancing with you and feel your emotions. When you are really hot, drop down and throw all your energy at the item like a lightning bolt!

Move the candle and, with the raw edge of one of the pieces of ginger, "draw" this on the musical item with ginger juice:

Repeat the verse above, then blow out the candle.

Soon you will be making beautiful music together. Don't forget
to light that candle when the music starts . . .

HOT PINK SPELL

Pink is the most neglected and dissed color in the world! Where would our bodies be without pink?! Yet pink gets little respect. Well, that is going to change right now! Use this to enchant anything pink you want to wear to cause a stir at work or play! Heads will turn and pink will be *the* color of the day after you walk in! Get "in the pink" and blow a few minds!

YOU WILL NEED
+ something very pink (blouse, shirt, pants, etc.)
+ a very pink rose

THE SPELL
The night before you want to wear the pink item, lay it out and stand over it, facing west.

Take the rose by the stem like a wand to make a long, slow continuous, clockwise spiral from as far west as you can reach to the center of the item.

As you make your spiral, think of blending white (male energy) with red (female energy) into pink, and say, as many times as you like:

Om vijaya shiva shakti namah!

Touch the rose to the item and repeat the mantra above one more time with all the energy you can. See pink energy flow into it. Then break apart the rose blossom and scatter the petals all over the item. Clap your hands three times, then go to bed!

The next day, shake off those petals, put on that pink thing, and go throw some sparks!

Hot Mail Spell

A love letter, card or note have all been the beginning of wild and torrid love affairs in history. People have died over love letters! It is so romantic and the postal service never takes advantage of this. The point is, nothing is more traditional than a "spelled" love letter or note. Here is a classic but still powerful way to send your love.

You Will Need
+ a love letter or note with envelope
+ a red scented candle
+ matches
+ a red apple
+ a red pen

THE SPELL

When you have written your note or card, sign it "Love," kiss it, and place it in the envelope. Light the candle and carefully wave the envelope through the fire three times, saying:

> IN MY WORDS, OH SEE
> HOW I BURN FOR THEE

Pick up the apple, take a bite and seal the envelope using the wet part of the inner apple, saying:

> IN MY WORDS, OH TOUCH
> HOW I LOVE THEE SO MUCH

On the back of the envelope, over the flap, use the red pen to draw a heart. Inside the heart draw an "X" inside an "O," like this:

Say:

İn my words, oh feel
With great love İ seal

Kiss it one more time—put a little feeling into it! Then blow
out the candle, eat the apple, and send that little Cupid's
arrow off. *Twang!* Expect a hot mail response . . . or, better
yet, a very special hand-delivered visit!

HOT PIE SPELL

What is yummier that a big, hot slice of pie? Okay, this is a spell to incite . . . well . . . amorous feelings in whoever eats it, so you do have to be a little careful. Still, the results are worth it, any way you slice it. This can be big fun at potlucks!

YOU WILL NEED
+ all the fixings for a nice apple pie
+ some real ground vanilla bean
+ ground cardamom
+ ground cloves

THE SPELL
The best time to work this is late Friday afternoon or evening, but any time or day is really fine. This is one lusty pie, so be careful whom you serve it to.

When mixing the filling (apples and sugar or honey), add the
following ingredients and then utter these words:

A half-teaspoon of ground vanilla:

Awaken the sense of smell
Full of sensuality
Awaken the hunger within
As I will so mote it be!

A half-teaspoon of ground cinnamon:

Awaken the sense of touch
Sensuous seed of a tree
Awaken the fires within
As I will so mote it be!

Three pinches of ground cloves:

AWAKEN THE SENSE OF TASTE
OF TONGUE AND BODY FREE
AWAKEN THE JOYS OF LOVE
AS I WILL SO MOTE IT BE!

Stir the filling again three times, saying:

BY WYRD THREE
SO MOTE IT BE!

Finish the crust, then cook it and serve it. You just might need
to leave the room for the *real* dessert, yum!

THE HOT FUDGE SUNDAY SPELL

You can imagine what *this* spell is about, and you are pretty
much right! Hold those thoughts! This spell is guaranteed to
sweeten up your Sundays and cure that sweet tooth!
Oh yes it will . . .

YOU WILL NEED
✦ a jar or bottle of truly excellent chocolate sauce.
You can even use chocolate liquor if you like!
Warm it before you begin the spell.
✦ a friend to play with
✦ your imagination

THE SPELL
You should do this on a bed or very comfortable sofa. You
may want to put a sheet down first.

Take out the chocolate sauce. Both of you should hold it, saying:

ELIXIR OF PASSION
ELIXIR OF HEAT
ENFLAME OUR LOVE
WE ARE WHAT WE EAT!
ZOS KIA!

Take turns using the chocolate sauce to paint a moon crescent on the forehead of the other person. Then, taking turns, sensuously lick and kiss the chocolate off your partner.

Next, each should draw a small sun in chocolate on the other's chest, and kiss or lick it off as before.

Then, each person should draw a little triangle around the belly-button of the other person, in turn, and kiss and lick it away.

Finally, each should place some on his or her tongue and then passionately kiss.

Each should now use his or her imagination and continue in the same manner . . . until most of the jar is gone or one or both of you are stuck to the floor!

You will become much, much closer and you have chocolate to thank for it!

HE'S HOT SPELL

Boys will be boys, and girls will be girls, and anyone can be anything he or she wants 'cause it is a new millennium! If there is a hot boy you want to dig you, do this little thing and stuff will happen. But beware! "Don't call up what you can't put down," as the old shamans once said. You may have someone who loves your butt long after you are bored with him! Looking for a girl instead? The next spell is for you!

You Will Need
+ the king of hearts from a new deck of cards
+ something sharp and gold-plated
+ a tall, thin red candle in a candle holder
+ matches

THE SPELL
Starting one week before the full moon, take out
everything you need.

Hold up the card and kiss it, saying:

BY MY LOVE
I NAME THEE MINE
COME TO ME
BY POWER DEVINE
OH ——— (PERSON'S NAME)
IT IS MY TIME!
MARITUS ADES DUM!

Scratch the initials of the loved one on the back of the card
with the sharp item. Place the card face up under
the candle holder.

On the candle, scratch this rune:

Then light the candle, saying:

YOU'LL NEVER BE FREE
UNTIL YOU COME TO ME
WE ARE ROYALTY
SO MAY IT BE!

Let it burn for a while and think deeply about what you desire,
then blow it out.

Do not move the candle or card!

For the next six days, light the candle and repeat the previous
verse, then think about your spell and blow it out.

On the night of the full moon, do the same thing, but let it
burn completely down.

Later, somehow, give the card to the object of your desire. If
he keeps it, you are good as gold and will soon have a new
special friend. If he doesn't keep it, it was not meant to be!
Toss that hook back into the river and go get a new candle!
Bonne chance!

She's Hot Spell

Here's one to get that gal . . .

You Will Need
+ the queen of hearts from a new deck of cards
+ something sharp made of silver or silver-plated
+ a short, squat red candle and a small bowl to put it in
+ matches

The Spell
Starting one week before the full moon, take out everything
you need.

Hold up the card and kiss it, saying:

BY MY LOVE
I NAME THEE MINE
COME TO ME
BY POWER DEVINE
OH ——— (PERSON'S NAME)
IT IS MY TIME!
MARITA ADES DUM!

Scratch the initials of the loved one on the back of the card
with the silver item. Place the card face up under the bowl
with the candle in it. On the candle, scratch this rune:

Then light the candle, saying:

> YOU'LL NEVER BE FREE
> UNTIL YOU COME TO ME
> WE ARE ROYALTY
> SO MAY IT BE!

Let it burn for a while and think deeply about what you desire, then blow it out.

Do not move the candle or card!

For the next six days, light the candle and repeat the previous verse, then think about your spell and blow it out.

On the night of the full moon, do the same thing, but let the candle burn completely down!

Later, somehow, give the card to the object of your desire. If she keeps it, you are in like a silver bullet and will soon have a new special friend. If she doesn't keep it, it was not meant to be! Toss that hook back into the river and go get a new candle! *Bonne chance!*

HOT STUFF SPELL

Desire is not always directed at fellow humans, is it? How
many times have you walked by a display window and
seen . . . something. You stop and your pulse rate jumps.
You *must* have it. You know what I'm talking about. When you
have a material desire, here is a little spell to fan the flames in
the right direction. It is true that you can't take it with you,
but you sure as heck can enjoy it while you're here!

YOU WILL NEED
+ a small novelty magnet (either with a hole in the
middle or looking like a small horseshoe)
+ a permanent red marker
+ some red cord (three feet is enough)
+ a small gold candle
+ matches

The Spell
On a Sunday night, as the moon is waxing, lay out the items
and face north.

With the marker, write these runes on the magnet
with the marker:

As you do so, say:

Sowilo fill with light
Draw which glitters bright
Tyr my desire fulfill
By my strength and will
Uruz bring me pleasure
Gift to me great treasure
Fehu flowing free
Bring great wealth to me!

Tie the cord to or through the magnet and then make a knot
so you can wear the magnet around your neck so it
touches your heart-center.

Light the candle and pass the magnet through the flame
four times, saying:

SOWILO, TYR, URUZ, FEHU
BRING ME RICHES THAT ARE MY DUE!

Then hold it in the flame one more second while intensely
visualizing what you want.

Hang it around your neck and wear it for at least three days.
Keep using it to attract your desire!

When you get what you want, keep the charm. You will always
desire something else, right?

HOT! HOT! HOT! SPELL

Look, love is so much about attitude, don't you think?
Otherwise, how could some people who are not all that
attractive always have tons of lovers flocking to them? They
have self-sexy-confidence and project an erotic aura that
attracts potential sweeties like a flame attracts moths. Want
that kind or aura? Try this spell and get yourself a broom
'cause you will be beating the "interested parties" away!

You Will Need
+ seven small candles that are the colors of the rainbow
(red, orange, yellow, green, blue, indigo, violet)
+ holders or plates to put them in
+ a small amount of good quality ylang-ylang oil
(another sexy scented oil will do)
+ matches

THE SPELL

Do this on a Sunday afternoon. Place the candles clockwise in a circle around you on the floor so they make a five-foot circle for you to stand in the middle of. Start at the east and lay them out in their holders in the order of colors mentioned. Then, clap your hands seven times and say:

> ALL THAT'S MEEK
> SAD OR GRAY
> I BANISH NOW!
> I INVOKE THE DAY!
> IRIS INVINCUS!

Take the oil in one hand and the matches in the other. Starting with the red candle at the east, put a little oil on the candle and light it. Do this with each candle, going in a clockwise direction, each time saying:

HOT HOT HOT
COLORS BURN BRIGHT
I'M HOT HOT HOT
I AM FILLED
WITH LIGHT!
IRIS INVINCUS!

When done, spin about seven times, seeing in your mind all the seven colors of the candles fly up and cover your body with a glowing rainbow! Then, put a dab of oil on the top of your head, your forehead, your throat, your heart, your belly button, your lower belly, and at the base of your spine. Each time breathe in deeply and see the rainbow colors fill you! You will be filled with great joyful energy!

Play in this rainbow circle as long as you like. When you feel like you are the hottest thing on the planet, then blow out the candles, beginning at the last one (violet) and going backward (counterclockwise) until you at last blow out the red one. Then clap your hands three times and say:

I am light
And so i'll stay
I go forth
To love and play!
Iris invincus!

Wow! Now you have a hot hot hot rainbow aura!
When you go out, see this hot aura flashing around you.
Now, go out and let your love light shine!

HOT ASTROLOGY SPELLS

Every idiot who thinks you're hot tells you their "sign," right? "Hey, beautiful, I'm a Taurrrrrrus, how about you?" Well, here's a chance to use it to your advantage, isn't that great? Want to get a new lover, get a line on an old lover, or keep that current one firmly on the love hook? Use the power of the stars! All you need is to find out his or her birth sign, and he or she will tell you that right off! Then cast the right astrology spell on the one you desire. Have fun and tell your friends. You can also check out your sign, and make that special pal put a spell on you—it's sexy and fun! Makes you starry-eyed . . .

Aries

Romance does not skip a beat with Aries. Hot, passionate feelings are the norm, and no one expresses them better then Aries. Setting just the right mood will bring the Ram around. Aries loves to be noticed—words of praise and ego boosting go straight from the ears to the heart. The trick to get Aries lovers started: Just listen to them. They love to be the center of attention, and they feel they've gotten yours if you look them directly in the eyes and stare them down. Here is a little spell to get your Aries into action.

You Will Need
+ a red rose
+ your favorite sexy incense
+ a music CD
+ matches

THE SPELL

Put the red rose on your pillow and light your favorite incense
while playing a new CD. While the music is playing, sit on the
bed and concentrate on absorbing deeply into your heart
what your Aries wants from you. Do this until the CD is
finished. When you see your sweetie, give him or her the rose
and CD. Watch Aries spring into action.

Taurus

Ah earthly delights, spring is just around the corner, magic is in the air, and you! It takes time for a Taurus to warm up and make a commitment. A Taurus has to feel secure and steady. Love is nothing a Taurus takes lightly. It's wise to be honest with a Taurus; he or she has a hard time forgiving any type of indiscretion. Nothing brings out the romance in the Taurus more than the simplicity of the earth. One way to get his or her attention is this little spell. Let magic bring your Taurus loved one around.

You Will Need
+ a red candle
+ matches
+ a potted primrose plant
+ an apple

THE SPELL

Light the red candle and stare into the flame visualizing that
as the flame goes higher, your love is burning twice as hot.
Take some of the earth from the potted plant and sprinkle it
on the apple. Brush it off, then, give the apple to your loved
one when he or she comes home and offer your sweetheart a
bite. Think Adam and Eve.

Gemini

It takes two to tango, and you have both of them on your mind! That is how it feels to love a Gemini! Which twin do you like and which one do you want to spend a hot date with? Your Gemini is two people in one, or so it seems. The trick with Gemini is that his dual hearts beat as one, but with twin desires.

To solve the mystery of Gemini is to understand what makes him or her stay and not flee. Offer your Gemini as much freedom as he or she wants, and you will be sure that he will not take it. Gemini just wants to know it is there. Gemini hearts desire poetry, so to get your Gemini to settle down to serious romance, try this love spell.

You Will Need

+ your favorite romantic poem
+ a blue pen
+ an empty journal

The Spell

Read your favorite poem out loud. It does not matter if the poem is one that you wrote or one that you just love. Now read the poem again, saying your and your love's name three times. Take the pen and write the poem in your love's journal, then give him or her the journal on some special day. Watch your Gemini respond with true love.

CANCER

Sweet Cancer loves to give and love you back! If you don't want your Cancer to be crabby, remember to celebrate all special days, especially Valentine's Day. He or she expects to be treated special on certain holidays. Your intended will give a lot to you, so you should be aware with Cancers that wining and dining can turn into whining and dividing, if you don't give back! While you're at it, write down all the other holidays you share together, like your first kiss, birthdays of pets, and anything else you might leave out. To keep your Cancer romantically inclined, nothing but the best will do. Try this little love spell before you go out to dinner.

YOU WILL NEED

For a woman:

+ matches
+ a white candle
+ a rose corsage
+ a box of chocolates

For a man:

+ matches
+ a white candle
+ a small bottle of musk cologne
+ a box of his favorite hard candy

THE SPELL

Before you go to your favorite little romantic restaurant, try this traditional love spell: Light the white candle and stare into the flame and whisper the following while holding the rose corsage and box of chocolates (or the cologne and the hard candy):

MY LOVE FOR YOU IS TRUE
AS ARE MY GIFTS TO YOU!

Blow out the candle, place the chocolates (or hard candy) on the bed (dessert!), and, when you meet, pin the rose on that lover (or anoint him with a bit of cologne) before you walk into the restaurant.

LEO

Leos welcome romantic holidays with a roar! Big-hearted Leos enjoy sharing their love with those who appreciate them. They need affection and admiration from people who they are involved with. Not to be taken lightly, they are loyal, fierce lovers who will let you know if you cross any boundaries. Leos love to plan for romantic interludes, but anything is romantic to a Leo. It is hard to outdo them in their arena. The trick is in letting them think it's their idea (give them plenty of praise) in picking out what you both like to do. To make the evening a success, try this spell.

You Will Need
+ two red candles
+ matches
+ red thread
+ a sewing needle

THE SPELL

Light the red candles facing east and wind the red thread
around both candles, saying:

THE TIES THAT BIND
ARE STRONG
WE ARE ONE WITH LOVE
MAY IT BIND US LONG!

Now take the sewing needle and lightly etch your initials
on one candle and your lover's on the other. Repeat the
invocation and blow out the candles. Give them to your
sweetheart as a present to burn over
romantic dinners at home.

Virgo

Simple perfection is the way to win a Virgo's heart. Your Virgo likes any displays of attention to be well thought out and well timed. Messy scenes or loud displays of affection will not do.

Quiet overtures of love and a peaceful setting invoke the power of passion in Virgo. Think places, not people, and make any gift you give *tasteful*, not gaudy! Virgos love a simple walk in the woods or an outing with a gourmet picnic. Your Virgo lover is a class act. Treat a Virgo like the rare jewel that he or she is and you will be repaid with years of devoted love. Try this simple spell to get the Virgo fires burning bright.

You Will Need
+ a postcard of a nearby romantic place
+ a red-ink pen
+ a crystal

THE SPELL

Hold the postcard in your hand and creatively visualize a romantic tête-à-tête. Then place the crystal on the postcard. Write you and your lover's name on the card with some pet names that you have for each other (if you have some). Then repeat his or her name eleven times along with the phrase "you are my jewel." Later give that loved one the "rock" and the postcard, the best place being at the same spot the postcard is from.

Libra

Romance, candlelight, soft music—what else does a Libra
need? Having the right surroundings are key, but attitude,
with Libra lovers, is even more important. There is nothing
worse than seeing all your well-laid plans go out the door if
your Libra feels stifled and hemmed in. Libras like space, so
whatever you do, don't plan on anyplace small and intimate.
Keep the conversation from anything political because Libras
love a good argument. Your Libra knows just what to do if the
place is right. Trust Libra and he or she will make any evening
shine. To keep the mood going all year long, try this
old family recipe.

You Will Need
- a pink candle
- matches
- a photo of the two of you
- a beautiful small journal

The Spell
Light the candle and say:

I light this candle to you from me
May we never disagree
Keep our love flame burning bright
Shining forever, day and night

Place the photo of the two of you in the journal and write down your dreams for the both of you on the first page and blow out the candle. Now get ready to go out on the town (you're with a Libra, silly, did you think you would get off cheaply?). Hand him or her the "dream book" at the right time. Ya got 'em!

Scorpio

Intensely focused Scorpios know what to do in romance. You
have to decide how hot *you* want the furnace of love to get!
Once you turn on their heat, there is no going back: Scorpios
are in charge, and they set the tone. To get your needs met
before you become consumed, you may want to set a couple
of ground rules. Scorpios are very honest; they will follow any
boundaries that you set. They make the rules, you set the
boundaries, and now the love can begin. To keep it fair, and
you with the upper hand, try this spell.

You Will Need
+ a strong perfume or cologne
+ a red sash
+ a selection of exotic and/or spicy candy
+ your favorite pleasurable beverage

THE SPELL

Place the perfume or cologne on the pulses of your body,
visualizing where you want to get kissed later. Now, tie the
red sash around your Scorpio's eyes and open the box of
candy. Take out one piece and place it in his mouth. Have him
guess what it is, and when he gets it right, kiss him hard. He
can only kiss you back where you placed your perfume. This is
sort of a sexy scavenger hunt. The blindfold shouldn't come
off until the right moment. You'll know. Later, toast your love
with your favorite beverage after you drop one piece of the
candy into each full glass.

Sagittarius

The sexy Sag is in his or her own professional league. Sags can have a short span on their fun-o'-meter; when they get bored, they move on. Don't end up being a poor sport—be on the winning team! When you are ready to play ball, Sag will be too. This will get action moving in the right direction for those who don't want to keep score. Try this magical spell to get your Sagittarius sweetie to stand up and cheer!

You Will Need

+ a sports shirt (any shirt with a team mascot that they like will do if they don't have a favorite)
+ a "sporty" cologne or after-bath splash
+ an orange candle
+ matches

The Spell

Take the sporty T-shirt and change it into a magical talisman
by doing the following:

First, get nude and think of your honey.

Next, spray some of the sporty cologne or perfume on you
and the shirt.

Finally, while looking in your bedroom mirror, light the candle
and say this invocation:

Pan of power and desire
Give me the one
Who sets me on fire

Now put on the jersey (nothing else, please!) and give your
partner the cologne as a gift. The jersey is for you to share, at
least for special nights when you both need a touchdown . . .

Capricorn

A traditional romantic offering of flowers and candy is just what Capricorn desires, but how do you make it special? Your Capricorn loves cocooning. A quiet place for just the two of you is perfect. Capricorns love staying home, so a homemade dinner served half-dressed gets their attention! Any way you look at it, your Capricorn responds well to anything you do with care. If it looks like you consider their feelings, then they respond with warmth and humor. It's nice to know that you have someone in your life who can give as well as take, hmm? Want a spell to get them good? Then try this one.

You Will Need
+ a blank card
+ some small decorations
+ a small piece of red velvet
+ drawing pens

+ scissors
+ a glue stick
+ romantic photos (or other pictures)
+ a red string

THE SPELL

Make an old-fashioned "I love you" card. Don't worry if the last time you made one was third grade. Your Capricorn will be the first to tell you that it's the thought that counts. Make sure there is a heart of red velvet on it somewhere. Add decorations or images that mean something to both of you. When done, kiss the red heart with all your might! Then place the finished card where your sweetheart will find it, attaching the red string to it. Tie the other end of the red string to your toe or to a present. Watch your Capricorn laugh and tell you how great you are. Have fun!

Aquarius

What makes your Aquarius tick? Aquarius loves the unconventional, so start with a hot e-mail card and work up from there. Aquarius loves surprises, and the more the merrier. An activity that includes a social gathering is what turns an Aquarius on, then quality time begins! Too much alone time makes an Aquarius a little nervous; they thrive on quality, not quantity, one-on-one time. Take your Aquarius out for something social and off-beat, and watch the fireworks. I bet you wondered where their passion was? It is for life! If you want to see more, try this spell.

You Will Need
+ balloons
+ ribbons of shiny material
+ lavender scent for a woman, lemon for a man

Blow up the balloons and tie the ribbons onto the balloons. Each time you finish a balloon say your lover's name and yours. Tie the balloons together.

Next, face west and spray the scent in the air. Then do the same for the next three directions, saying:

I SALUTE THE WEST (SAY YOUR LOVER'S NAME)
I SALUTE THE EAST (SAY YOUR LOVER'S NAME)
I SALUTE THE NORTH (SAY YOUR LOVER'S NAME)
I SALUTE THE SOUTH (SAY YOUR LOVER'S NAME)

Now in the middle say:

I SALUTE (HIS OR HER NAME AND YOURS)
IN ENDLESS WAYS
MAY OUR LOVE REMAIN THROUGH ALL OUR DAYS

Now, surprise! Give the balloons to your sweetheart in a public place and make a big deal out of it! Love, baby!

PISCES

Sensitive Pisces loves baubles and clever little gorgeous things. It is always wise to add to any of their many collections on special days. They ooze with romance anytime they are around water, so to get your fishy to dive in, lead them to any watery source. A dinner along the waterfront is divine, but always make sure that you are dressed properly and that you have reservations. Pisces don't like to wait, and they like to look like they belong in fancy surroundings. They're sensitive to their environment, so make sure that the place is in a good neighborhood. Pisces tend to want to save the less fortunate and may spend the date listening to other people's romantic problems or feeling sorry for the less fortunate. Here's a spell to keep Pisces focused on you!

YOU WILL NEED
+ a pink candle
+ a white candle
+ a red candle
+ a shallow pan
+ a little pure water
+ matches

THE SPELL

Place the three candles in the pan standing up, and add some water. Light the candles and hold your Pisces' hand (or think about doing that) and say:

YOU AND ME
PEACE AND LOVE
FOREVER TO BE
OUR LOVE FOREVER
LIKE THE SEA!

Begin in a loud voice and slow down to a whisper, then blow out the candle. Use some of the water to wash up with. Add the rest to your lover's bath or shower. Now you both feel romantic and ready for what the evening will bring!

About the Author

Sophia is a professional psychic, astrologer, and spiritual teacher with more than twenty-five years of experience, both in the United States and abroad. She was taught how to tap her psychic powers by her grandparents when she was a child. At the age of three she began her study of psychic reading, psychic healing, and spell casting. She has written a regular column called "Emerging Women" for the *New Times* and maintains a thriving practice as a professional reader and teacher. She currently carries on the family tradition in a yurt in a wooded corner of Seattle, Washington.